DISCOVERING AFRICA

SOUTHERN
AFRICA

Countries of Southern Africa

Angola, Botswana, Lesotho, Malawi, Mozambique, Namibia, South Africa, Swaziland, Zambia, Zimbabwe.

DISCOVERING AFRICA

SOUTHERN
AFRICA

Annelise Hobbs

MASON CREST

Mason Crest
450 Parkway Drive, Suite D
Broomall, PA 19008
www.masoncrest.com

Cataloging-in-Publication Data on file with the Library of
Congress.

Printed and bound in the United States of America.

First printing
9 8 7 6 5 4 3 2 1

ISBN: 978-1-4222-3719-9
Series ISBN: 978-1-4222-3715-1
ebook ISBN: 978-1-4222-8070-6
ebook series ISBN: 978-1-4222-8066-9

Produced by Regency House Publishing Limited
The Manor House
High Street
Buntingford
Hertfordshire
SG9 9AB
United Kingdom

www.regencyhousepublishing.com

Text copyright © 2017 Regency House Publishing
Limited/Annelise Hobbs

TITLES IN THE DISCOVERING AFRICA
SERIES:

A Concise History of Africa
East Africa
North and Central Africa
Southern Africa
West Africa

CONTENTS

KEY ICONS TO LOOK FOR:

Words to Understand: These words with their easy-to-understand definitions will increase the reader's understanding of the text, while building vocabulary skills.

Sidebars: This boxed material within the main text allows readers to build knowledge, gain insights, explore possibilities, and broaden their perspectives by weaving together additional information to provide realistic and holistic perspectives.

Text-Dependent Questions: These questions send the reader back to the text for more careful attention to the evidence presented there.

Sand dunes at Sossusvlei which is part of the Namib-Naukluft National Park encompassing part of the Namib desert in Namibia.

ANGOLA

A republic located on the western coast of southern Africa, Angola has land borders with Congo and DR Congo to the north, Zambia to the east, and Namibia to the south. The Atlantic coastal area is flat, unhealthy and unproductive, though there is a vast fertile plateau beyond.

Angola became a possession of Portugal in the 16th century, when it

Words to Understand

Crude oil: Petroleum as it occurs naturally in its unrefined state.

Malnutrition: An unbalanced nutrition resulting from not eating enough, or enough healthy food.

Marxist: A political, economic, and social theory advocated by Marx leading to the establishment of a classless society.

OPPOSITE: Residential dwellings in Luanda, the capital city of Angola.

BELOW: A map of Angola.

supplied slaves to Brazil. In the 1950s nationalists began to demand independence; the Popular Movement for the Liberation of Angola (MPLA) was formed,

drawing its support from mestizos and the Mbundu tribe. In 1961 the MPLA led a revolt in Luanda that was quashed by Portuguese troops, and other nationalist movements

developed between different ethnic groups. Independence was granted in 1975 but a power struggle developed among rival nationalist forces. The **Marxist** MPLA formed a government, but troops of the National Union for the Total Independence of Angola (UNITA) launched a civil war that lasted for 16 years. A treaty was signed in 1991 and multi-party elections were held the following year.

Civil strife continued, however, when the MPLA, now no longer Marxist, was victorious and UNITA would not accept the result. In accord with the Lusaka Protocol, a government of national unity was formed in 1994, with leaders from both parties. Dos Santos remained president but UNITA's Jonas Savimbi rejected the vice-presidency, which led to continued fighting. This resulted in UN sanctions being imposed on UNITA in 1997, but the fighting did not stop. In 2002 government forces killed Savimbi and a ceasefire was agreed. Over the coming years, although the political situation of the country stablized, regular democratic processes were not established until the elections of 2009 and 2012.

To most people, Angola is synonymous with bloodshed, its association with Portugal and the acquisition of diamonds and **crude**

oil being responsible for this in equal measure. But Angola's present economy is being driven by its oil sector, with record oil prices and rising petroleum production giving growth averages of more than 15 percent per annum. A post-war

ABOVE: Angolan dwellings built in traditional style.

LEFT: The Catholic cathedral of Lubango.

OVERLEAF: The beautiful Kalandula Falls are situated on the Lucala River. They are 344 feet (105m) high and 1,300 feet (400m) wide. They are one of the largest waterfalls by volume in Africa.

Tundavala Gap

Tundavala Gap is situated on the rim of the great escarpment called Serra da Leba. It is located some 12 miles (18km) from the city of Lubango, in Huíla province, Angola.

The escarpment marks the western limit of Bié Plateau. The altitude at the rim exceeds 7,217 feet (2,200m), while the plain below is approximately 3,937 feet (1,200m) lower. The impressive view from the gap stretches for miles. The rugged terrain is popular with climbers and hikers.

reconstruction boom and resettlement of displaced persons has also led to high rates of growth in construction and agriculture, although much of the country's infrastructure is still damaged or undeveloped from the long civil war. In 2016 Angola was hit by drought, causing high food prices and **malnutrition**.

Text-Dependent Questions

1. What natural resource drives Angola's economy?

2. How long did Angola's civil war last?

3. What caused malnutrition in Angola in 2016?

BOTSWANA

A landlocked country of southern Africa, Botswana lies to the north of South Africa. Most of the country is covered by the Kalahari Desert, though there are areas where cattle are grazed, and much of the rest is covered by the salt pans of the Okavango Swamp in the north-west, which is the world's largest inland delta.

Inhabited by Sotho people and by San nomadic **bushmen** in the Kalahari Desert, Bechuanaland was a British protectorate from 1885. It became a **republic** within the Commonwealth in 1966, when it adopted the name Botswana. Politically, it has remained remarkably stable and prosperous, having the good fortune to be an important producer of diamonds as well as other minerals. The country also has extensive game reserves and wildlife parks, which attract many tourists. The Okavango delta and Chobe National park are particularly exclusive.

Botswana has one of the world's highest known rates of HIV/AIDS infection, but also one of Africa's most progressive and comprehensive programs for dealing with the disease.

Words to Understand

Bushmen: Groups of peoples who live by hunting and foraging in southern Africa.

Landlocked: A country enclosed by land.

Republic: A country that is governed by elected representatives.

LEFT: Lilac-breasted roller (*Coracias caudatus*), Botswana's national bird, Chobe National Park.

OPPOSITE: A map of Botswana.

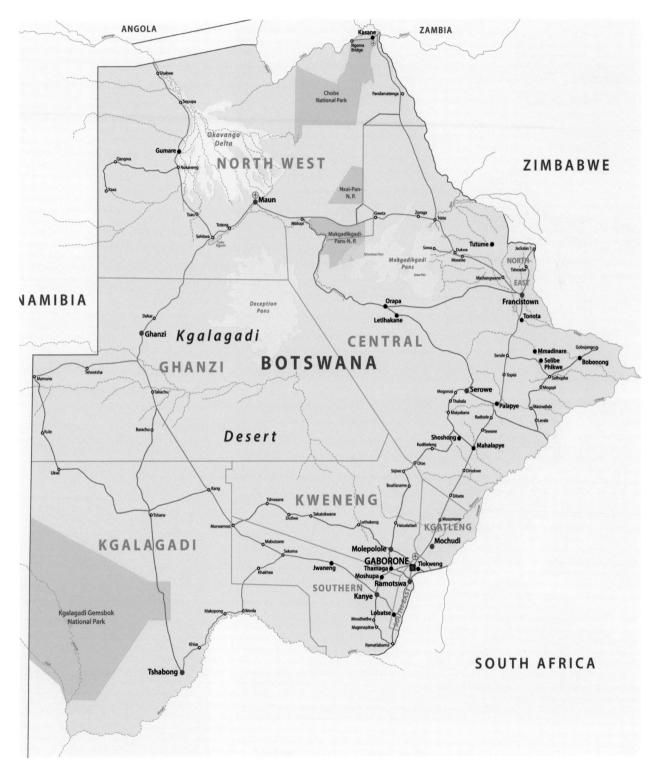

TOP: Two young Hippopotamuses, (*Hippopotamus amphibius*) play fighting.

ABOVE: The Lechwe (*Kobus leche*) is a common sight in the Okavango Delta.

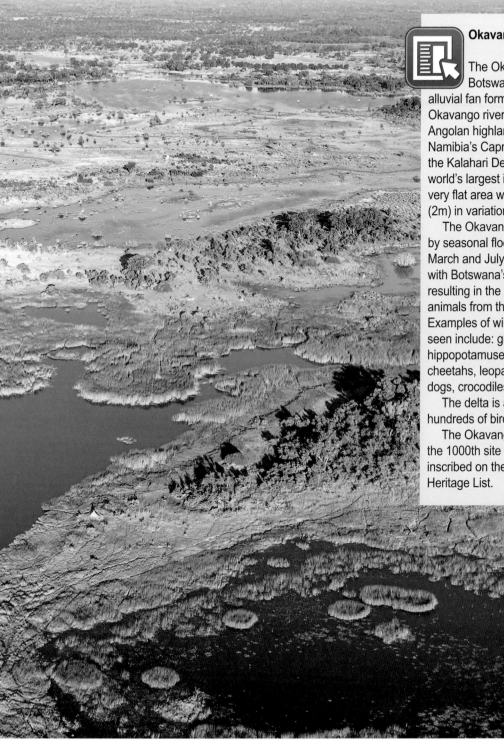

Okavango Delta

The Okavango Delta in Botswana is a very large alluvial fan formed where the Okavango river flows from the Angolan highlands, across Namibia's Caprivi Strip and into the Kalahari Desert. It is the world's largest inland delta. It is a very flat area with less than 7 feet (2m) in variation.

The Okavango Delta is affected by seasonal flooding between March and July. This coincides with Botswana's dry season resulting in the migrations of animals from the hinterland. Examples of wildlife that can be seen include: giraffes, hippopotamuses, buffalos, lions, cheetahs, leopards, hyenas, wild dogs, crocodiles, and antelopes.

The delta is also a santuary for hundreds of bird species.

The Okavango Delta became the 1000th site to be officially inscribed on the UNESCO World Heritage List.

Head of both state and government since April 1, 2008 is President Seretse Khama Ian Khama, the first-born son of Sir Seretse Khama (the country's foremost independence leader from 1966–1980).

ABOVE: Mokoro safari in Okavango Delta, Botswana.

OPPOSITE: Lioness (*Panthera leo*) with cubs in early morning light, Kalahari Desert.

Text-Dependent Questions

1. What is the name of Botswana's desert?

2. Who is Botswana's current president?

3. Why is Botswana politically stable?

LESOTHO

A mountainous, landlocked country, Lesotho forms an enclave within South Africa. There are areas where the valleys have been flooded by the headwaters of the Orange River, causing bogginess and an excess of surface water. The range of the Drakensberg Mountains lies to the south-east.

The Sotho nation was founded by Moshoshoe I, who united the nomadic tribesmen to fight the Zulus in the 1820s. During the years that followed, a losing battle with the encroaching **Boer** settlers was fought, which led what was now Basutoland to seek the protection of the British in 1868. Basutoland subsequently became part of the British Cape Colony and was eventually under Britain's direct rule.

During the years that followed, **Basutoland** lost fertile land to South Africa, with the result that most of

ABOVE: Botanical Gardens at Katse Dam. It is concrete arch dam on the Malibamat'so river and is Africa's second largest dam. It is part of the Lesotho Highlands Water Project, which will eventually include five large dams in remote rural areas.

OPPOSITE: A map of Lesotho.

Words to Understand

Basutoland: A former name for Lesotho.

Boer: A South African person of Dutch descent.

Migrant: A person who travels to another country or place, usually to find work.

the population ended up working in the mines or on the farms of South Africa, which continues to this day. Basutoland became an independent kingdom within the Commonwealth in 1966, when its name was changed to Lesotho, the Paramount Chief becoming head of state as King Moshoshoe II. In 1970, the prime minister, Chief Leabua Jonathan, annulled the first post-independence election, refusing to cede power to the Basuto Congress Party (BCP) and imprisoning its leadership. Continuing conflict for many years

ended in a military coup in 1986, when executive powers were given to Moshoeshoe II, who until that time had been a king in name only. Within a few years, however, he was forced into exile. In 1990, he was deposed and his son Letsie III became king.

In 1992, the BCP won the first multi-party elections, when military rule came to an end. Letsie III tried unsuccessfully to have his father restored as king and in 1994, backed by the military, staged a coup to overthrow the BCP. Eventually, Moshoeshoe II was restored but died in a car accident in 1996, when his son again became king and head of state. The BCP, which had also been restored, was now split by leadership disputes. A new ruling party, the LCD, was formed in 1997 under the leadership of Prime Minister Ntsu Mokhehle as a split from the BCP. On February 21, 1998, Pakalitha Mosisili was elected leader

BELOW: A Basotho man wearing a traditional blanket leading a horse.

OPPOSITE: A Basotho village in the highlands of Maluti Mountains, near Ribaneng, Malealea.

of the LCD after Mokhehle chose to step down due to poor health. Pakalitha Mosisili remains as prime minster today, despite losing an election in 2012 when Thomas Thabane became prime minister, but following elections in 2015 he became prime minister once again.

Text-Dependent Questions

1. Who founded the Sotho nation?

2. Who is Lesotho's current prime minister?

3. What important resource does Lesotho sell to South Africa?

Maletsunyane Falls

Maletsunyane Falls is 630 feet (192m) high. It is one of the world's highest waterfalls. It is located near the town of Semonkong, meaning site of smoke, which also is named after the falls. The waterfall is on the Maletsunyane river. The falls are an interesting tourist attraction and can be reached in four hours by bus from Maseru.

Completion of a major hydro-electric facility in January 1998 permitted the sale of water to South Africa, generating valuable income for Lesotho, which produces about 90 percent of its own electricity. The people of Lesotho, however, still rely on subsistence agriculture and their livestock, also on the earnings of **migrant** workers, despite the fact that their numbers are declining. A small manufacturing base has developed, however, that qualifies Lesotho for the trade benefits contained in the Africa Growth and Opportunity Act. The extreme inequality in the distribution of income continues as a major problem.

MALAWI

A small country of south-central Africa, lying in the Great Rift Valley, Malawi is essentially a plateau, apart from Lake Malawi (Nyasa), which drains into the Zambezi via the Shire River. Lake Malawi covers half the country, and extends almost its entire length, forming Malawi's borders with Tanzania and Mozambique; Malawi

Words to Understand

Bauxite: An impure, clay-like substance that is the source of aluminium.

Corruption: Illegal or dishonest behavior by people in power such as government officials.

Vice president: An officer next in rank to a president.

OPPOSITE: Lake Malawi, also known as Lake Nyasa in Tanzania and Lago Niassa in Mozambique, is an African Great Lake and the southernmost lake in the East African rift system, located between Malawi, Mozambique, and Tanzania.

RIGHT: A map of Malawi.

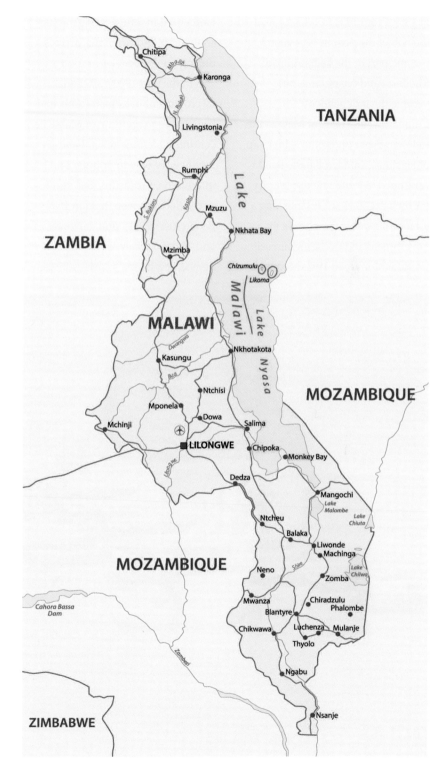

shares the lake with both countries. Mozambique also borders Malawi to the south and south-west, giving way to Zambia in the west.

Malawi grew from what was once a trader and missionary route to the Zambezi river. In the east, the plateau attains 3,000 feet (1000m), reaching 8,000 feet (2500m) on the Nyika Plateau in the north, and rising to 9,850 feet (3000m) in the south-east.

The first Europeans to visit the area were the Portuguese, who began to arrive in the 17th century. By the late 19th century, however, they had begun to have ideas of linking the territory with the Portuguese colonies of Mozambique and Angola. The British objected and made the area a British protectorate from 1891; it was known as Nyasaland from 1907.

Until then, the difficulty of the terrain and the ferocity of warring tribes prevented any real exploration of the country, although David Livingstone did reach Lake Malawi in 1859. From 1953 to 1963, against the will of the people, Nyasaland became part of the Federation of Rhodesia and Nyasaland, but became the independent Commonwealth state of Malawi the following year under the leadership of Hastings Kamazu Banda. Banda continued to dominate the country for the next 30 years, establishing a totalitarian one-party system of government and declaring himself president for life in 1971. More than half a million refugees, fleeing the civil war in Mozambique, arrived during the 1980s.

In the mid 1990s, after an improvement in human rights had been made a condition of Malawi's continuing famine relief, Banda finally gave way to popular and international pressure, and multi-party elections were held in 1994. Banda lost the election, however, and Malawi received its first taste of democracy. Banda's successor was

BELOW: Fishing boats on Lake Malawi.

Bakili Muluzi, who proved to be less oppressive, though there were accusations of **corruption** within the government. He was succeeded by Binguwa Mutharika in May 2004. However, his predecessor still has a hand in running their shared political party, which causes something of a power struggle

Nyika Plateau

Known for its wildlife, the Nyika Plateau lies in northern Malawi and has a small portion in north eastern Zambia. The highest point being 8,546 feet (2,605m) at Nganda Peak. It is roughly a diamond in shape, with a long north-south axis of about 55 miles (90km), and an east-west axis of about 31 miles (50km). It towers above Lake Malawi (elevation 1,558 feet 475m), and the towns of Livingstonia and Chilumba. Its well-defined north-west escarpment rises about 2,296 feet (700m) above the north-eastern extremity of the Luangwa Valley, and its similarly prominent south-east escarpment rises about 3,280 feet (1,000m) above the south Rukuru river valley.

between the two. Mutharika made efforts to eradicate corruption which led to several high-level arrests but no actual convictions. Mutharika went on to win a second term in 2009 and continued on as president until his death in 2012. He was succeded by **vice president** Joyce Banda. Malawi's current president is Peter Mutharika who won the presidential election in 2014. In the same year Malawi celebrated 50 years of independence.

Malawi is one of the world's poorest countries. Poverty is a continuing cause for concern and tens of thousands die of AIDS each year, although a program to combat the scourge was launched in 2004. In 2014 President Peter Mutharika said that on average Malawians were poorer than under colonial rule.

Malawi has few natural resources, and is a country prone to natural disasters, when food aid is inevitably required. Subsistence agriculture is the main activity, but tea and tobacco are exported and there are reserves of uranium, **bauxite**, and coal that remain to be exploited. Nevertheless, there is much to admire in Malawi's lakes, mountains, and forests, and its national parks and game reserves continue to attract visitors.

RIGHT: Mount Mulanje is a large mountain rising sharply from the surrounding plains of Chiradzulu in the south of Malawi. It is situated 41 miles (65km) east of Blantyre. It has a maximum elevation of 9,849 feet (3,002m) at its highest point which is Sapitwa Peak.

Text-Dependent Questions

1. Geographically, what is the significance of Lake Malawi?

2. Who were the first Europeans to visit Malawi?

3. In what year did Malawi celebrate 50 years of independence?

MOZAMBIQUE

A country on the eastern coast of southern Africa, Mozambique has a coastline on the Mozambique Channel and the Indian Ocean. It has land borders with Tanzania, Malawi, Zambia, Zimbabwe, South Africa, and Swaziland. A wide coastal plain, through which many rivers flow to the sea, including the Zambezi and Limpopo, rises to highlands of up to 8,000 feet

Words to Understand

Exodus: A situation in which many people depart from a place at the same time.

Famine: A situation where food is so scarce that people do not have enough to eat.

Natural resource: Something naturally occurring that is valuable and benefical to humans.

LEFT: The Samora Machel Statue is a bronze sculpture located in the center of Praça da Independência in Maputo, Mozambique. The statue depicts Samora Machel, military, revolutionary, and the first president of Mozambique.

OPPOSITE: A map of Mozambique.

(2450m); rain forests of ebony and ironwood teem with wildlife. The only real harbor is the capital, Maputo, formerly the city of Lourenço Marques.

The indigenous people of Mozambique are from the Bantu tribes, but by the 10th century Arab traders in ivory and gold had established themselves along the coast. After the area had been visited by Vasco da Gama in 1498, however, the Portuguese began to arrive and colonization began in 1505, formalized in 1910; in the interim, huge plantations were built.

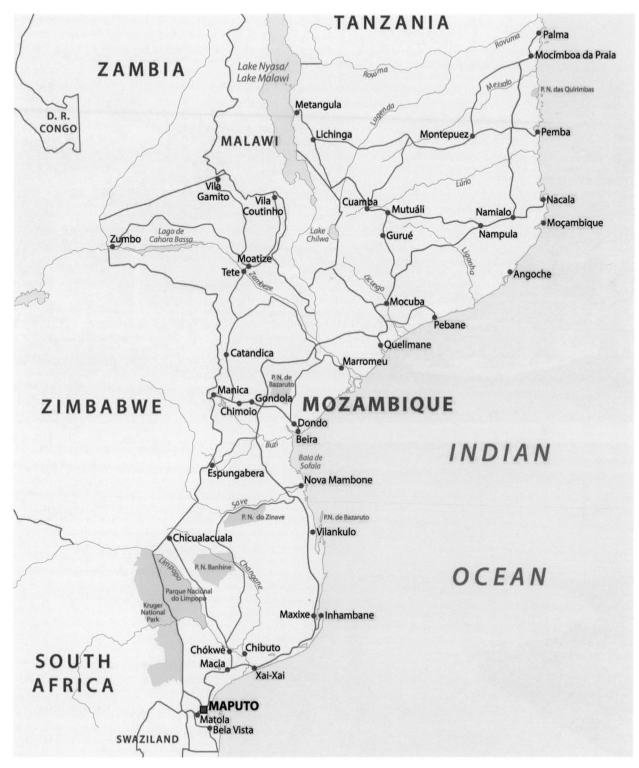

Mozambique was a center of the slave trade in the 18th and 19th centuries. It achieved independence from Portugal in 1975, after a ten-year struggle by the FRELIMO (Frente de Libertação de Moçambique) liberation movement, which resulted in a mass **exodus** of

ABOVE: Maputo, capital of Mozambique.

LEFT: Sand dunes, Bazaruto Island.

OPPOSITE: Traditional sailboat on the coast of Mozambique.

Portuguese settlers and the draining of the country's resources.

The new FRELIMO government, with the FRELIMO leader Samora Machel its first president, established a one-party Communist state; it also assisted other liberation movements in Rhodesia (Zimbabwe) and South Africa, bringing them into conflict with the Mozambique National Resistance Movement (RENAMO) opposition. Civil war raged from 1977–92, when thousands of people lost their lives.

Samora Machel died in 1986 and was succeeded by Joachim Chissano. In 1989 FRELIMO abandoned Marxism and a multi-party system

Mozambique

was adopted. In 1992, following a period of severe drought and **famine**, a UN-negotiated peace agreement was signed. In 2000 the Zambezi and Limpopo rivers flooded, leaving vast areas of the country under water, making almost a million people homeless and destroying much of the country's infrastructure. In 2004, Chissano

stood down after 18 years in office, and was succeeded by Armando Emilio Guebuza who continued on as president until 2015. Mozambique's current president is Filipe Nyusi.

At independence, Mozambique was one of the world's poorest countries, and socialist mismanagement and a brutal civil

BELOW: Traditional Mozambique village in the mountains.

OVERLEAF: Aerial view of coastal waters, forests, and lagoon in Mozambique.

war only served to exacerbate the situation. In 1987, the government embarked on a series of reforms designed to stabilize the economy. These, combined with assistance

Gorongosa National Park

First established as a hunting reserve in 1920, and then a National Park in 1960 under Portuguese colonial rule, Gorongosa National Park is at the southern end of the Great African Rift Valley in central Mozambique. The park covers over 1,544 square miles (4,000km^2) and includes the valley floor and parts of the surrounding plateaux. Rivers originate from nearby Mount Gorongosa causing seasonal flooding and waterlogging of the valley below. This creates a distinctive and unique ecosystem. Today the park is protected by the government, and although the park is fragile, there have been some successes. The park lacks the density of wildlife it once had, but many species are starting to thrive again.

Pictured here are two Impala (*Aepyceros melampus*).

from abroad, and with political stability since the multi-party elections in 1994, have led to dramatic improvements in the country's growth. Inflation was reduced to single figures during the late 1990s, and although it returned to double figures in 2000–06. In recent years Mozambique has attracted investment into its vast **natural resources** including natural gas, coal, and titanium and consequently, the country is now performing strongly.

Text-Dependent Questions

1. What tribes were the indigenous people of Mozambique from?

2. How long did the civil war last for?

3. What rivers flooded in 2000 leaving vast areas under water?

NAMIBIA

Namibia is an arid country, situated in south-west Africa. The Namib Desert lies along its coastline on the Atlantic Ocean in the west, while the Kalahari Desert extends into Botswana in the east. It has other land borders with Angola and Zambia to the north and South

Words to Understand

Mandate: A formal order to do something.

Offshore: Located in the ocean a distance from the shore.

Pegged: A predetermined level that a price can be fixed at.

Namib-Naukluft National Park

The Namib-Naukluft National Park encompasses part of the Namib Desert (considered the world's oldest desert) and the Naukluft mountain range. With an overall area of 19,216 square miles (49,768km²), the Namib-Naukluft is the largest game park in Africa and the fourth largest in the world. The most well-known area of the park is Sossusvlei, which is the main visitor attraction in Namibia. The park is home to many animals including: Hartman's mountain zebra, kudu, oryx, springbok, warthog, ostrich, and many insect, bird, and reptile species. Along with the park's other attractions, visitors will experience the spectacular and classic desert scenery of apricot-colored dunes.

OPPOSITE: Wild desert coastline of the Atlantic Ocean at the Namib-Naukluft National Park.

BELOW: A map of Namibia.

Africa to the south. The central plateau is where the capital, Windhoek, is located, while to the north lies an alluvial plain and the marshlands of the Caprivi Strip.

The San were the original inhabitants of the country, but were eventually replaced by Bantu-speakers, such as the Ovambo, Kavango, and Herero. The area was annexed by German South-West Africa in 1884, when it was the scene of the Herero rebellion, which was quashed with unnecessary brutality.

In 1920 South-West Africa, as Namibia was then called, was mandated to South Africa by the League of Nations; South Africa, however, continued to administer the country after the **mandate** had expired in 1964, despite international censure.

In 1966, the SWAPO (Marxist South-West African People's

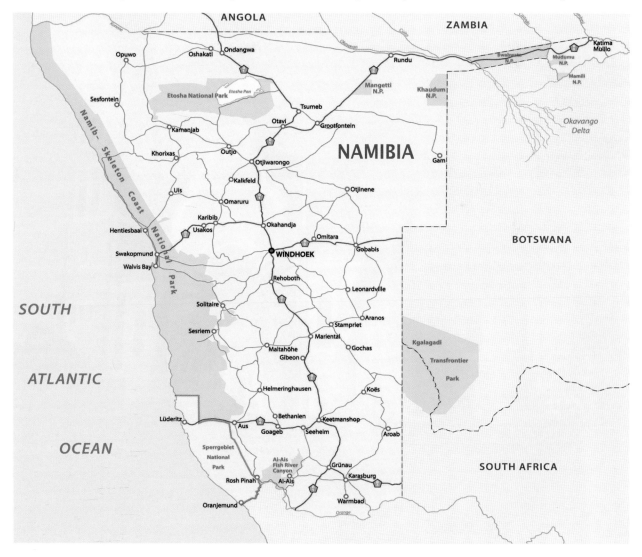

OPPOSITE: Christ Church is a historic landmark and Lutheran church in Windhoek.

BELOW: Oryx (*Oryx gazella*) are a common sight in the savanna grasslands in Etosha National Park.

Organization) guerrilla movement launched a war of independence, but it was not until 1988 that South Africa, in accordance with a UN peace plan, agreed to withdraw. Namibia became fully independent in 1990 and has been governed by

SWAPO ever since. Head of state from 2004–2014 was President Hifikepunye Pohamba; he replaced Sam Nujoma, who had led the country during its first 14 years of self-rule. In 2015 President Hifikepunye Pohamba was awarded

the five million dollar Mo Ibrahim prize for African leadership. The award is given to an elected leader who governs well. Namibia's current president is Hage Geingog.

Where it exists, Namibia has good grazing, and cattle, goats, and sheep are reared, yielding valuable skins. **Offshore** there is good fishing and crops are grown here and there. The Namibian economy is closely linked to South Africa, with the Namibian dollar **pegged** one-to-one to the South African rand. Namibia's mineral wealth acounts for the bulk of its exports, with fish production and the mining of zinc, copper, uranium, and silver spurring growth.

RIGHT: Granite rock formations north of the Brandberg mountain in the Namib Desert.

Text-Dependent Questions

1. What is Namibia's capital city?

2. What is the Mo Ibrahim prize for?

3. What other country's economy is Namibia's linked to?

SOUTH AFRICA

A country occupying the southern extremity of the African continent, most of South Africa is covered by Highveld, a natural grassland that gives way in the south to the lesser plateaux of the Little and Great Karroo. These are bordered to the south and east by the ranges of the Swarteberge, Sneeuberge, Stormberge, and Drakensberg mountains, then by a lowland coastal margin. In Transvaal, the veld is crossed by the long ridge of Witwatersrand and its goldfields, on which Johannesburg stands, while Table Mountain, at 3,550 feet (1082m) overlooks the city of Cape Town in the extreme south-west. South Africa has coastlines on the South Atlantic and Indian

BELOW: An aerial view of Cape Town and its football stadium. Table Mountain is in the background.

OPPOSITE: A map of South Africa.

Oceans and land borders with Namibia, Botswana, Zimbabwe, Mozambique, and Swaziland; Lesotho is an enclave to the south-

east, and lies totally encompassed within South African territory.

In 1652 the Dutch East India Company established the Cape of Good Hope as a port of call for shipping on the way to the Indies. The area had expanded by the 18th century into a Dutch possession, by which time half the population were

Words to Understand

Afrikaner: A person born or raised in South Africa whose first language is Afrikaans.

Subjugation: Forced submission.

Segregation: The practice of keeping people of different races separate from each other.

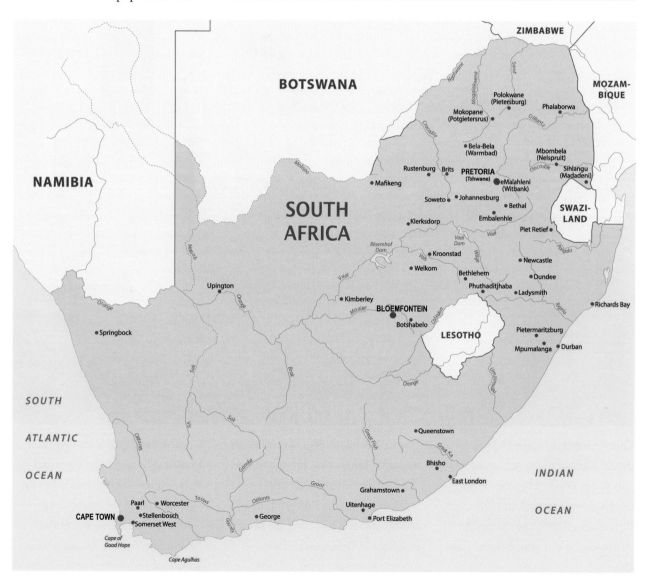

Cape Coloreds or Cape Malays, descendants of indigenous peoples and slaves imported by the Dutch, who had intermarried. In 1797 Britain seized the Cape during the Anglo-Dutch War and annexed Cape Colony in 1805. In 1836 some 10,000 Boers (Dutch farmers), in an attempt to escape British rule, set out on the "Great Trek," meeting fierce resistance from the Zulu kingdom on the way, and founding the Boer republics of Transvaal and the Orange Free State from 1852–54.

The discovery of diamonds in Kimberley and gold in Transvaal attracted prospectors and led to the **subjugation** of the natives and conflict with the Dutch farming community. In 1877 Britain annexed Transvaal and overcame the Zulus in

the Zulu War of 1879. In the First Boer or South African War, Transvaal Boers defeated the British at Majuba in 1881 and regained their independence. Denial of the rights of citizenship to British immigrants in Transvaal, and the imperialist ambitions of Cecil Rhodes, led to the Jameson Raid and the Second Boer War (1899–1902). The Boers, led by Jan Smuts and Louis Botha, continued to resist until the British, by reason of superior numbers, seized the Boer republics at last.

ABOVE LEFT: Pretoria is in the northern part of Gauteng province. It is one of the country's three capital cities.

ABOVE: The Hillbrow Tower (JG Strijdom Tower) is a tall tower located in the suburb of Hillbrow in Johannesburg. In 2010 it was decorated for the Football (soccer) World Cup.

In 1910 the Union of South Africa was formed, comprising the Cape of Good Hope, Natal, Orange Free State, and Transvaal, with Botha as prime minister. In 1912 the African National Congress (ANC) was formed to improve the rights of the majority black population. The outbreak of the First World War was marked by a Boer rebellion that was speedily crushed by Smuts. German South-West Africa (Namibia) was occupied and later mandated to the Union, and Union forces served in East Africa and France. Between the wars there were alternating periods when the (Boer) Nationalist Party,

under General Hertzog (who wished to further racial **segregation** and sever ties with the British Empire), and the South African Party under Smuts (who wished to maintain the Commonwealth connection), were in power. They merged to form the United Party in 1934, in an attempt to reconcile **Afrikaner**- and English-speaking whites, but split over the Union's entry to the Second World War on the side of the Allies, the right-wing National Party having sympathies with Nazi Germany.

In 1948, when the National Party under Daniel Malan came to power, a stringent policy of

apartheid (separate development of the races) was adopted. (This was continued under Johannes Strijdom (1954–58), Hendrik Verwoerd (1958–66), B.J. Vorster (1966–78) and P.J. Botha (1978–89.) In 1950 the entire population was classified by race and blacks and whites were segregated. The ANC responded

ABOVE: Durban is a coastal city in eastern South Africa's KwaZulu-Natal province.

OPPOSITE: The Blyde River Canyon is a significant natural feature in South Africa. It is located in Mpumalanga and forms the northern part of the Drakensberg escarpment.

with a campaign of civil disobedience, culminating in the massacre at Sharpville in 1960, when 70 black demonstrators were killed and the ANC was banned. The following year, in the face of Commonwealth opposition to apartheid, South Africa left the Commonwealth, adopting the status of a republic.

In 1964 the ANC leader, Nelson Mandela, was sentenced to life

Text-Dependent Questions

1. What city does Table Mountain overlook?

2. When was the Union of South Africa formed?

3. What natural resources are mined in South Africa?

imprisonment; detention without trial was introduced three years later. In the 1970s over three million people were forcibly resettled in black "homelands" and many were killed in clashes between black

protesters and security forces in Soweto. A new constitution in 1984 gave segregated representation to coloreds and Asians, but continued to exclude blacks. Growing violence in black townships led to a state of emergency from 1985–1990, and sanctions were imposed by the Commonwealth and the USA.

In 1989 F.W. de Klerk succeeded Botha as president; public facilities were desegregated, and many ANC activists were released. The following year, the ban on the ANC was lifted and Mandela was released. In 1991 the remaining apartheid laws were repealed and

Nelson Mandela

Nelson Mandela (1918–2013) was a South African activist and former president. He was the country's first black head of state in its first democratic election. During the 1940s he led both peaceful and armed protests against the white minority's oppressive regime, for which he was sent to prison for 27 years. In 1994 he was elected president in a sweeping victory. Once head of state he focused on dismantling the legacy of apartheid by tackling institutionalized racism and fostering racial reconciliation.

sanctions were lifted, though clashes continued between the ANC and Chief Buthelezi's Zulu Inkatha movement.

In the first multi-racial elections in 1994, Mandela became president and membership of the Commonwealth was restored. In 1995 a Truth and Reconciliation Commission, headed by Archbishop Desmond Tutu, began to investigate crimes committed under apartheid. In 1999 Mandela retired from the presidency and was succeeded by

Thabo Mbeki until 2009 when he resigned over allegations that he interfered in a corruption case. South Africa's current president is Jacob Zuma.

Daunting economic problems still exist, hangovers from the apartheid era, and include poverty, high unemployment and lack of empowerment in disadvantaged groups; AIDS and crime are also major problems. On the other hand, South Africa has abundant natural resources, with mining forming the

basis of its economy. It also has well-developed financial, communications, energy and transport sections, as well as a stock exchange that is among the largest in the world. It is the world's largest producer of platinum, gold and chromium, and produces diamonds and machinery.

ABOVE: Falls on the Crocodile River. The river traverses Mpumalanga province.

SWAZILAND

A landlocked country of south-east Africa, Swaziland takes its name from the Swazi, a Bantu tribe. It is bordered on the north, west and south by South Africa, and to the east by the Lebombo Mountains and Mozambique. The terrain consists of a central valley (Middleveld), with the eastern Drakensberg Mountains (Highveld) to the west and the Lowveld to the east.

Words to Understand

Dynasty: A powerful family of rulers who rule over a country for a long period of time.

Hereditary: Holding a position or title that was passed down by an older relative.

Overgrazing: To allow animals to graze land to a point that the vegetation cover becomes damaged.

LEFT: The Maguga Dam is situated on the Komati River in Hhohho. It is 377 feet (115m) high and is located 7 miles (11km) south of Piggs Peak.

OPPOSITE: A map of Swaziland.

Swaziland has one of the oldest monarchies on the African continent. Towards the end of the 16th century, according to tradition, Ngwane II, a Bantu chief, founded a **dynasty** that dominated the indigenous Nguni and Sotho tribes. By the beginning of the 19th century, his descendant, Sobhuza I, had established a powerful Swazi kingdom, and by the mid 1880s the warrior king, Mswati I, ruled an area three times the size of the present country. In 1882 gold was discovered in the north-east, attracting fortune-hunters from Europe; these

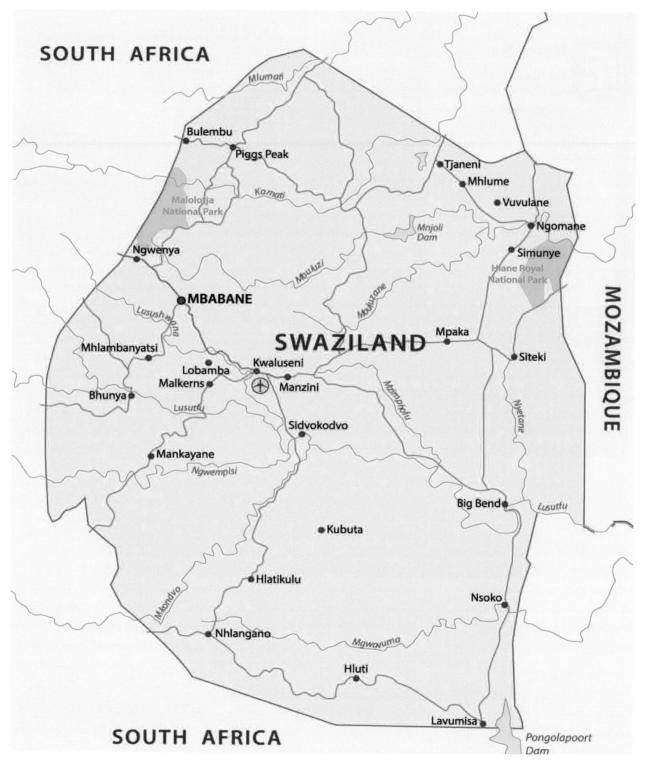

Ngwenya Mine

The Ngwenya Mine is located on Bomvu Ridge, north-west of Mbabane. This mine is considered to be the world's oldest perhaps dating back 42,000 years. The haematite ore deposit was used in the Middle Stone Age to extract red ochre, while in later times the deposit was mined for iron smelting and iron ore export. On the same site is a sacred pool used by local people. It is believed that the waters can cure illnesses.

succeeded in gaining land concessions, usually by coercion.

In 1894 Swaziland came under the joint rulership of Britain and the Boer republic of Transvaal. Following the South African War of 1899–1902, Swaziland, against the wishes of South Africa, became a British protectorate in 1903. In 1922 King Sobhuza II ascended the throne, and when Swaziland became an independent kingdom within the Commonwealth in 1968, he became **hereditary** head of state. In 1973,

however, the struggle began between a totalitarian monarchy and those seeking democracy. The king reacted by suspending the constitution, banning political activity, and assuming absolute power, substituting a traditional tribal system for parlimentary rule. He died in 1982, when one of his numerous wives became regent until the crown prince came of age. The regent, Queen Dzeliwe, was ousted by a younger wife the following year as real power passed to the prime

minister, Prince Bhekimpi Dlamini. In 1986 the crown prince came to the throne as King Mswati III; he grudgingly reinstated a parliamentary system in 1990, following agitation from students and workers, and promised political reform. In 1993 elections of candidates were held for the first time, and again five years later.

A constitution came into effect in 2006, but political parties remain banned, although the African United Democratic Party tried

ABOVE: Sibebe Rock is a granite mountain in Swaziland located 6.2 miles (10km) from the capital city Mbabane. It is the second-largest monolith in the world, second only to Ayers Rock in Australia. It rises 1148 feet (350m) above the valley of the Mbuluzi River. Sibebe Rock is a popular tourist attaction and a haven for birds, some of which are endangered. Guided walking trails are available to take tourists to the summit.

Text-Dependent Questions

1. What century does Swaziland's monarchy date back to?

2. Who is Swaziland's current prime minister?

3. What percentage of the population relies on subsistence farming?

unsuccessfully to register as an official political party in mid 2006. Talks over the constitution broke down between the government and progressive groups in 2007. The current prime minister is Barnabas Sibusiso Dlamini.

Being practically an enclave of South Africa, Swaziland is heavily dependent on its powerful neighbor, both for imports and exports, and the money Swazi workers in South Africa send home is vital to their families. Over 80 percent of the population relies on subsistence agriculture, since the exhaustion of iron ore reserves in 1978, with sugar and wood pulp the chief products. **Overgrazing**, soil depletion and drought has added to its challenges. It has a high incidence of HIV/AIDS but now appears to be stemming the pace of new infections.

LEFT: White rhinoceroses or square-lipped rhinoceroses (*Ceratotherium simum*) in Hlane Royal National Park. It is the only rhino species that is threatened but not endangered.

ZAMBIA

A landlocked republic of south-central Africa, Zambia, formerly Northern Rhodesia, is divided from Zimbabwe and Botswana in the south by the Zambezi river, from which Zambia takes its name. It is also bordered by Mozambique and Malawi to the east, Tanzania to the north-east, DR Congo to the north, Angola to the west, and Namibia to the south. The terrain mostly consists of a vast expanse of high plateaux. In the south the Zambezi occupies a low-lying rift valley of rugged **escarpments**, and the Muchinga Mountains lie to the north.

There were major influxes of Bantu-speaking immigrants from the 12th century and others followed into the 19th century, including the Luba and Lunda tribes of DR Congo and Angola, which were joined by Ngoni peoples from the south. The area was visited by Portuguese in the 18th century and by missionaries, traders, and explorers in the mid 19th century. In 1855, the

Zambezi River

The Zambezi is the fourth largest river system in Africa. It is the longest east flowing river in Africa and the largest flowing into the Indian Ocean from Africa. The 1,599 mile (2,574km) long river rises in north-west Zambia and flows through eastern Angola, along the eastern border of Namibia and the northern border of Botswana, then along the border between Zambia and Zimbabwe to Mozambique, where it crosses the country to empty into the Indian Ocean. Unlike many other important rivers, the Zambezi is less developed along its banks and many parts of it enjoy protected status.

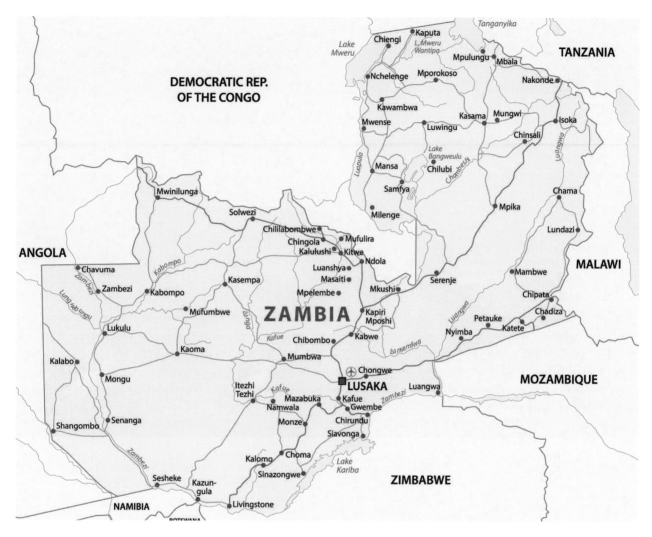

ABOVE: A map of Zambia.

Scottish missionary and explorer, David Livingstone, was the first European to see the magnificent waterfalls on the Zambezi river, naming them after Queen Victoria. In 1888 Cecil Rhodes and his British South Africa Company obtained mineral rights from local chiefs,

Words to Understand

Defector: A person who abandons a country, political party, or organization to go over to a rival or enemy.

Escarpment: A steep slope or cliff that separates two flatter areas.

Humanism: A system of values that focuses on the idea that people are basically good.

drew northern and southern Rhodesia into the British sphere of influence, and gave the country his name. Southern Rhodesia was formally annexed and granted self-government in 1923, and Northern Rhodesia became a British protectorate in 1924. Local rebellions were quashed and mining began in the north-eastern Copperbelt in 1934.

In 1953, both Rhodesias joined Nyasaland (now Malawi) to form the Federation of Rhodesia and Nyasaland, Northern Rhodesia

becoming independent within the Commonwealth as Zambia after the federation was dissolved in 1963. (Southern Rhodesia became independent as Rhodesia in 1965, becoming Zimbabwe in 1979.)

Kenneth Kaunda had led the campaign for independence and was Zambia's first president from 1964 to 1991. He tried to bring a measure of **humanism** and co-operation to his government, and there was increased control of the economy. The constitution of 1973 provided for a National Assembly and a

consultative House of Chiefs. It also made his United National Independence Party (UNIP) the only political party, where before there

ABOVE: Elephant (*Loxodonta africana*) with calf near the Zambezi river. Lower Zambezi National Park, Zambia.

OPPOSITE: A flock of grey crowned cranes (*Balearica regulorum*) in South Luangwa National Park. They occur in dry savanna in Africa south of the Sahara, although they nest in somewhat wetter habitats. They can also be found in marshes, cultivated lands, and grassy flatlands near rivers and lakes in Uganda and Kenya and as far south as South Africa.

had been three, the UNIP, the African National Congress (ANC), and the United Progressive Party (UPP).

Growing opposition to the UNIP's monopoly of power gave rise to the Movement for Multi-party Democracy (MMD), which included UNIP **defectors** and labor leaders. This resulted in the end of one-party rule in 1991 and victory for the MMD, when Frederick Chiluba was elected president. The subsequent re-election of Chiluba in 1996 was achieved after Kaunda was effectively barred from further elections by a change in constitution.

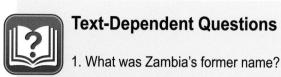

Text-Dependent Questions

1. What was Zambia's former name?

2. What was David Livingstone's nationality?

3. When did Zambia gain independence?

In 1997 there was an abortive anti-government coup; Kaunda was suspected and arrested, but charges were subsequently dropped. The election of President Levy Mwanawasa in 2001 was also widely challenged; Mwanawasa began an anti-corruption campaign in 2002, which resulted in the prosecution of former President Chiluba and many of his supporters. Mwanawasa was re-elected in 2006 in an election that was deemed free and fair, however in 2008 he died from the effects of a

Zambia

stroke. The current president is Edgar Lungu who won the election in 2015.

In spite of its considerable copper wealth, Zambia has been facing major problems following independence in 1964. There were few Zambians capable or educated enough to run the country, and the economy had been founded on foreign expertise. Zambia was also affected by its involvement in Zimbabwe's struggle for independence (1965–1979). In 1975 world copper prices collapsed, further devastating the economy, with the result that Zambia is currently one of the world's poorest nations and much of its population is decimated by disease. However, copper prices have lately recovered and the government has accepted that diversification is required if it is to exploit Zambia's other resources, such as agriculture, oil, tourism, gemstones, and hydropower.

LEFT: The awe-inspiring and astounding grandeur of the Victoria Falls on the Zambezi river. One of the world's greatest natural wonders, the falls are part of two national parks, Mosi-oa-Tunya National Park in Zambia and Victoria Falls National Park in Zimbabwe. The falls are just over a mile wide. As the explorer David Livingstone remarked, "scenes so lovely must have been gazed upon by angels in their flight."

ZIMBABWE

Alandlocked country of south-central Africa, lying between the Zimbabwe and Limpopo rivers, Zimbabwe is bordered by Zambia to the north, Mozambique to the east, South Africa to the south, and Botswana to the west. The broad central plateau (Highveld) rises in the north-east to 5,000 feet (1500m), and highlands along the eastern border rise to 8,504 feet (2592m) at Mount Inyangani.

Words to Understand

Austerity: A economic situation where money is in short supply and it is only spent on things that are essential.

Hyperinflation: A very rapid rate of inflation causing a rapid increase in the price of goods and services.

Transvaal: A former province in north-eastern South Africa.

OPPOSITE: High-rise buildings in Harare, Zimbabwe's capital city.

BELOW: A map of Zimbabwe.

The area was occupied by Bantu peoples, notably Shona, who began to settle around 2,000 years ago. By the 11th century Great Zimbabwe, the center of the Shona culture, was famous for its gold and metalwork, but had noticeably declined by the

1400s. In 1837 the warlike Ndebele (Matabele), after unsuccessful skirmishes with the Boers in the **Transvaal**, seized Shona land in the west, where Matabeleland was established. In 1888, Cecil Rhodes obtained mineral rights from King

Lobengula, and the territory became a British protectorate, administered by the British South Africa Company. From 1895 Matabeleland, Mashonaland, and Zambia, across the Zambezi river, were collectively known as Rhodesia. Thereafter, white colonization was encouraged and the country's precious metal and mineral resources were systematically plundered.

In 1923 the area south of the Zambezi became a self-governing colony. From 1933 to 1953, a policy of black exclusion from government was followed, and white immigration had nearly doubled the population by the 1950s. Southern and Northern Rhodesia became members of the Federation of Rhodesia and Nyasaland (now Malawi) from 1953 to 1963. In 1961, meanwhile, the Zimbabwe African People's Union (ZAPU) had been formed by Joshua Nkomo. In 1963, following the dissolution of the federation and contrary to British policy that African majority rule

ABOVE: Great Zimbabwe is a ruined Iron Age city in the south-eastern hills of Zimbabwe near Lake Mutirikwe and the town of Masvingo. The central area of ruins extend to 200 acres (80 hectares). Great Zimbabwe was the center of a thriving trading empire from the 11th to the 15th century. Great Zimbabwe is a UNESCO World Heritage Site.

OPPOSITE: The Domboshava rocks are an interesting series of granite formations made by natural eroson in the province of Mashonaland East.

should come first, the white minority demanded independence.

That year, the Zimbabwe African National Union (ZANU) was formed by Robert Mugabe. Southern Rhodesia was known simply as Rhodesia from 1964, following the creation of Zambia (Northern Rhodesia): the white nationalist leader, Ian Smith, became prime minister that year, rejecting the British terms on which independence should be based. In 1965, unilateral independence was proclaimed, which Britain declared illegal. Negotiations between the two came to nothing, despite the imposition of UN sanctions, and Rhodesia declared itself a republic in 1969, which was not recognized internationally.

Resistance to white rule intensified from the late 1960s, characterized by attacks on white farmers. In 1974 Mugabe and Nkomo were released from prison, having been incarcerated since 1964, and formed the Patriotic Front (PF) ito fight the Smith regime. With his regime near to collapse, Smith signed an accord with Mugabe, Nkomo and Bishop Abel Muzorewa in 1978, though the Muzorewa government soon faltered and guerrilla warfare intensified. At the height of the civil war, 1,000 white Rhodesians were leaving the country every month, taking vital capital with them. Following the Lancaster House Agreement of 1979, Rhodesia was granted transitional independence as the Republic of Zimbabwe (Zimbabwe-Rhodesia), when a new "majority" constitution was formed, still favoring whites.

In 1980 Zimbabwe received full independence from Britain, having

RIGHT: Runde river in Gonarezhou National Park.

BELOW: Young African leopard (*Panthera pardus shortidgei*), Hwange National Park.

agreed to a transition to African majority rule. The Reverend Canaan Banana became president and Robert Mugabe prime minister. In 1982 Nkomo was ousted from the cabinet, which sparked fighting between ZAPU and the ruling ZANU; this was marked by the genocide of the Ndebele by ZANU's infamous Fifth Brigade, which resulted in Nkomo's capitulation and the merger of ZAPU with the ZANU Patriotic Front.

Gonarezhou National Park

Gonarezhou National Park situated is in the south-eastern lowveld of Zimbabwe. It is located in a relatively remote corner of Masvingo Province, south of Chimanimani along the Mozambique border. Gonarezhou is famous for its elephants. "Gonarezhou" means "place of many elephants."

In 1984 the principle of a one-party state was agreed, with Mugabe abrogating all power to himself three years later. In 1992 Mugabe announced the drought and famine in southern Africa a national disaster. This compounded the country's debt and led to IMF adjustment of the economy and a program of **austerity** causing further hardship. The government's chaotic land reforms had also badly damaged the farming sector, which was once a major source of export revenue. In 2001 2,900 white farmers, whose farms had been

ABOVE: Lake Kariba Dam is a hydroelectric dam providing electricity to Zimbabwe and Zambia. Each country has its own power station, the southern one belonging to Zimbabwe and the northern to Zambia.

Text-Dependent Questions

What is the Shona culture famous for?

Why did the EU impose sanctions in 2002?

Who is Zimbabwe's current president?

targeted for seizure and redistribution, were ordered to stop work under threat of imprisonment. This resulted in no crops being produced, which led to Zimbabwe's worst food shortages in 60 years, in a situation already exacerbated by drought.

Meanwhile, Mugabe had been re-elected president in 1996, following which bans on strikes and political gatherings were issued, and projected land reforms sparked violent demonstrations. In 2000 veterans of the war of independence, with government approval, began to invade and claim white-owned farms without compensating their owners. In 2002 the EU imposed sanctions following the expulsion of observers sent to monitor the general elections; ignoring international condemnation, Mugabe rigged the 2002 presidential election to ensure his re-election. In 2003 Zimbabwe formally withdrew from the Commonwealth. In June 2007 Mugabe placed price controls on all basic commodities, causing panic buying and leaving store shelves empty for months.

Zimbabwe held elections on March 29, 2008, the major candidates being the incumbent president, Robert Mugabe, Morgan Tsvangirai of the Movement for Democratic Change (MDC), and Simba Makoni, an independent. Because of Zimbabwe's dire economic situation, the election was expected to provide Mugabe with his toughest electoral challenge to date, but no official results were announced for more than a month after the election. The failure to release results was strongly criticized by the MDC, which unsuccessfully sought an order from the High Court that would force their release. An independent projection placed Tsvangirai in the lead, but without the majority needed to avoid a second round. The MDC declared that Tsvangirai had won a narrow majority in the first round and at first refused to participate in any further round.

ZANU-PF announced that Mugabe would participate in a second round, after alleging that some electoral officials, in collusion with the MDC, had fraudulently reduced Mugabe's score, as a result

Zimbabwe

of which a recount was conducted. After the recount and the verification of the results, the Zimbabwe Electoral Commission (ZEC) announced on May 2 that Tsvangirai had won 47.9 percent and Mugabe 43.2 percent of the votes, thereby necessitating a run-off which was held the following month. Finally, Mugabe was declared the winner. By September, Mugabe and Tsvangirai signed a power-sharing agreement where Tsvangirai was sworn in as prime minister and remained so until 2013. President Mugabe is still Zimbabwe's leader today.

Zimbabwe has one of the highest incidence of HIV/AIDS in the world, which continues to drain

BELOW: Acacia tree (*Acacia tortilis*) in Hwange National Park.

RIGHT: Matobo National Park forms the core of the Matobo Hills, an area of gravity defying granite domes, spires, and balancing rock formations which have been hewn out of the solid granite plateau over 2,000 million years ago. The park is also home to many endangered animal species.

resources, as did its involvement in DR Congo's war (1998–2002). Despite all Zimbabwe's challenges, the economy of the country is now growing, although poor harvests and low diamond prices have hindered more rapid development. Dollarization in early 2009 allowed other currencies to be used locally ending **hyperinflation**.

Index

PHOTOGRAPHIC ACKNOWLEDGEMENTS

All images in this book are supplied under license from © Shutterstock.com.

The content of this book was first published as *AFRICA*.

ABOUT THE AUTHOR
Annelise Hobbs

After completing her Classical studies, Annelise Hobbs became a librarian, working in a busy area of central London frequented by local authors and university students as well as the public itself. Eventually, she decided to use her extensive knowledge, and particularly her interest in travel, art, and architecture, to help in her research as an editor, inevitably progressing to writing books herself.

FIND OUT MORE:

Websites

● **Lonely Planet**
www.lonelyplanet.com

● **Maps of Africa**
www.worldatlas.com

● **National Geographic**
travel.nationalgeographic.com

● **United Nations Educational, Scientific and Cultural Organization**
http://whc.unesco.org

Further Reading by Mason Crest

AFRICA PROGRESS AND PROBLEMS
13 VOLUMES | 112 PAGES
Africa is a complex and diverse continent, and its more than 50 countries provide a study in contrasts: democracy and despotism, immense wealth and crushing poverty, modernism and traditionalism, peaceful communities and raging civil wars. The books in the AFRICA: PROGRESS AND PROBLEMS series take a close look at many of the major issues in Africa today, such as AIDS, poverty, government corruption, ethnic and religious tension, educational opportunities, and overcrowding. *2014 copyright*

THE EVOLUTION OF AFRICA'S MAJOR NATIONS
26 VOLUMES | 80 PAGES
Africa, with its rich natural resources and its incredible poverty, is a continent of contradictions. Each book in this series examines the historical and current situation of a particular African nation. Readers will learn about each country's history, geography, government, economy, cultures, and communities. *2013 copyright*